KINGS AND QUEENS

HOW TO BECOME A RULER

In ancient times, you could become a ruler by being descended from a powerful leader, by winning an important battle or by overthrowing the previous ruler.

In time, titles like 'king' became the right of the eldest son. But since 2013, whichever prince or princess is born first becomes king or queen.

I'm in charge now!

Ouch!

MEET OUR NEW KING

His Majesty King Charles III came to the throne on 8 September 2022 immediately on the death of Queen Elizabeth II.

God save The King!

Charles is proclaimed King.

KING CHARLES III

Charles III was born in 1948. When his mother became Queen in 1952, it made him heir to the throne. At the age of nine Charles was made Prince of Wales. He held this title for 64 years until he became King!

FIND OUT MORE about King Charles III on page 47

BRAVERY, GENEROSITY AND SUCCESS

Every year, the government honours men, women and young people for personal bravery, raising money for charities and success in sport, music, art and entertainment. The Royal Family presents them with medals in a ceremony called an investiture.

Charles's wife, Camilla, is The Queen Consort. Together they support many charities and organisations.

An investiture medal

And don't be late!

DOs AND DON'Ts
Imagine you're going to receive an award from The King. Put a cross by things you SHOULDN'T do:

- [ ] Trip over
- [ ] Wear dirty trainers
- [ ] Bow and curtsy

A CORONATION

ELIZABETH II
Elizabeth II was crowned queen in June 1953 not long after the Second World War had ended. Many bomb-damaged buildings were still in ruins and some foods were still rationed.

HERE SHE COMES!
People came from all over the world to watch the procession from Buckingham Palace to Westminster Abbey where she was crowned.

Doesn't she look beautiful!

I can't see!

It's raining – but who cares!

We've camped out all night to get the best view

4

FIND OUT MORE about Elizabeth II on pages 23, 39

THE CROWN JEWELS

Queen Mary, Princess Elizabeth's grannie

King George VI

Queen Elizabeth, Princess Elizabeth's mother

Princess Elizabeth

Princess Margaret

This photograph shows George VI (Elizabeth II's father) after his Coronation in 1937. Princess Elizabeth, aged 11, wrote a letter to her parents saying:

'At the end, the service got rather boring as it was all prayers. Grannie and I were looking to see how many more pages to the end ...'

After William II was shot and killed while out hunting in 1100, his brother Henry was super quick to be crowned. VERY suspicious!

Get me a fast horse!

The Coronation is an ancient religious ceremony during which kings and queens make sacred promises.

The Crown Jewels are a special collection of priceless objects used in the ceremony. They are kept safe in the Tower of London.

SPARKLERS!

♦ St Edward's Crown is decorated with **444** precious stones.

♦ The Imperial State Crown is set with 2,868 diamonds, 17 sapphires, 5 rubies, 11 emeralds and 269 pearls.

St Edward's Crown is made of solid gold and only used in Coronations.

The Imperial State Crown is worn when leaving Westminster Abbey after the Coronation.

In 1216, King John lost all his treasure when he and his army crossed treacherous marshes. Could it still be there?

Woo-hoo!

A rumour said Henry IV's crown blew off during his Coronation in 1399. A bad sign?

And then ...

Yes

No!

Never!

The Sovereign's Sceptre is set with the largest diamond in the world.

LEARNING ON THE JOB

In the Middle Ages, some rulers became king or queen when they were very young. Advisers governed the country for them until they were old enough to rule themselves. Then they had to learn FAST!

PARLIAMENT

The Plantagenet kings and queens, who ruled from 1154 to 1485, met with important people to discuss problems. But rulers still had the final word. These meetings were called Parliament from the French word 'parler' meaning 'to talk'.

Bishops, barons and judges sit beside the king in Parliament.

Well, I think you're wrong

Rubbish!

Whatever they say I have the last word

I don't agree

Richard II

FIND OUT MORE about Parliament on pages 30, 35

A BIG CHALLENGE

Richard II was 10 when he was crowned king in 1377. He was only 14 when thousands of angry peasants invaded London and headed for the Tower of London where Richard and his court were staying.

Fairer wages for all!

Down with high taxes!

MASSIVE COURAGE!

Showing great courage, Richard arranged to meet Wat Tyler, the leader of the rebels. But Wat was killed by the Mayor of London before he got the chance to speak to the king. A SERIOUSLY dangerous situation! The mob could have easily killed Richard, but he promised to help and persuaded them to go home.

To the Tower!

BETRAYED!

Sadly, as soon as Richard returned to the Tower, he broke his promise and many peasants were captured and hanged. Was Richard showing his true character? He certainly turned out to be an unpopular ruler.

He promised me a carrot

I promise to help

9

INNOCENT VICTIMS

Some young rulers didn't stand a chance – they were victims of advisers who had sneaky plans of their own.

Now ... how do I make the princes disappear?

A WICKED UNCLE

Edward V became king in 1483 aged 12. His uncle Richard, Duke of Gloucester, was made his adviser. Richard claimed that Edward and his younger brother were not the true sons of their father, Edward IV.

He imprisoned them in the Tower of London and had himself crowned Richard III. The young princes were never seen again.

BONES DISCOVERED

In 1674, the bones of two boys aged about 10 and 12 were found in a box buried at the Tower of London. Could these have been the princes?

Richard III

FIND OUT MORE about Richard III on pages 18–19

A TEENAGE VICTIM

Lady Jane Grey had a rival to the throne, Henry VIII's daughter, Mary (later Mary I). Jane reigned for just nine days before being arrested for treason with her husband, Lord Guilford Darnley. Later, they were both beheaded on the orders of Mary's powerful supporters.

Lady Jane Grey was executed at the Tower of London in 1554.

She is only 16!

CAN YOU SPOT?
◆ The executioner
◆ The chaplain guiding Jane to the block
◆ Jane's lady-in-waiting who has fainted

WARRIOR KINGS

The Middle Ages were a time when warrior kings rode into battle on great war horses at the head of their armies.

WILLIAM THE CONQUEROR

William, Duke of Normandy, inherited lands in France when he was only seven. By the time he was 20 he was known as a brilliant but cruel warrior who won all his battles and captured all the castles he besieged.

> Je suis le King of the Castle

PROMISES, PROMISES

William had been promised the English crown by Edward the Confessor. But as soon as Edward was dead Harold Godwinson, Edward's brother-in-law, had himself crowned king.

William was FURIOUS! He assembled his army and invaded England. On 14 October 1066, Harold was killed in the Battle of Hastings. William I was crowned king on Christmas Day that year.

> Raaaaaasp!

> Booooo!

FIND OUT MORE about Windsor Castle on page 45

12

William built
Windsor Castle to
show the English
who was boss.

RICHARD THE LIONHEART

Richard I is one of England's great heroes.
He was crowned in 1189 but spent most of
his reign fighting in the Crusades. These were
wars in which Christians and Muslims battled
for control of sacred lands in the Middle East.
Richard's great enemy was Saladin.

Saladin

Richard I

SALADIN

Saladin is the Western name of
Salah al Din Yusuf ibn Ayyub, the
Muslim sultan of Egypt, Syria and
Yemen. Like Richard, he was famous
for his skills on the battlefield.

WARRIOR QUEENS

Queens didn't lead their armies into battle. But they did wear their own armour, command their soldiers in warfare and defend their castles under siege.

She's escaping!

EMPRESS MATILDA

When Henry I died in 1135, his daughter Matilda should have become queen. But powerful barons wanted a king and backed his easy-going nephew Stephen instead.

HUH!

Matilda wasn't going to stand for that! Stephen was crowned king in 1135 but Matilda carried on fighting for the crown for nearly 20 years.

Get her!

See ya!

ESCAPE!

One winter, Stephen's army imprisoned Matilda in Oxford Castle close to the River Thames. She put on a white cloak, climbed out and, with three of her knights, escaped across the frozen river to safety.

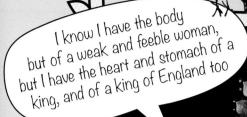

I know I have the body but of a weak and feeble woman, but I have the heart and stomach of a king, and of a king of England too

Queen Elizabeth's speech inspired her troops over 400 years ago. Do you think it would work today?

QUEEN ELIZABETH I

In 1588, the Spanish Armada threatened to invade England by sea. Elizabeth I met her troops at Tilbury Fort, near the mouth of the River Thames. Mounted on a fine horse and dressed to look like Athena, the Greek goddess of war, she delivered an inspiring speech. The invasion never happened. **RESULT!**

FIND OUT MORE about Elizabeth I on pages 24, 28–29

THE STUFF OF LEGENDS

When the Plantagenet kings and queens ruled about 700 years ago, England and France were at war so often it was called the Hundred Years' War.

ACTION IN FRANCE

Edward III's mother Isabella was French. She thought Edward had a better claim to the French crown than the French king. So Edward III, his son, Edward the Black Prince, and later, Henry V fought great battles in France.

We are the champions!

THE BATTLE OF AGINCOURT

In 1415 Henry V defeated a French army three times the size of his own at Agincourt. The battle was won through the skill of English and Welsh archers.

The Battle of Agincourt

CAN YOU SPOT?
◆ Henry V wearing the royal coat of arms
◆ An archer
◆ War horses
◆ Dead bodies

This silver groat was a day's pay for an archer. It was worth four old pennies (about £100 in today's money).

It's nothing, keep going!

WAR HORSE!

Kings rode into battle on war horses big and strong enough to carry a man in full armour.

Hands free for fighting

Henry V fought his first battle aged 16. An arrow struck his face and he was scarred for life.

Horse responds to pressure from legs.

War horses could bite, kick and trample on fallen enemies.

A TUG OF WAR

The Wars of the Roses (1455–85) was a bitter quarrel between two branches of the royal family – the House of Lancaster and the House of York. Both families wanted the Crown.

Arrrrrghhh!!!

THE BATTLE OF BOSWORTH

After 30 years of fighting, Richard III (the House of York) was knocked off his horse and killed at the Battle of Bosworth in Leicestershire. He was the last warrior king to be killed in battle. His death ended the Wars of the Roses.

Henry Tudor (House of Lancaster) was later crowned Henry VII in Westminster Abbey.

FIND OUT MORE about Richard III on page 10

THE TUDOR ROSE

Henry's family badge was a red rose. He married Elizabeth of York, whose family badge was a white rose. Henry combined the two badges to make the Tudor Rose.

THE KING IN THE CAR PARK

In 2012 Richard's body was discovered underneath a modern car park. It had been built over the ruins of a monastery where Richard was first buried in a hastily dug grave.

POWER TO THE PEOPLE!

King John who ruled from 1199 to 1216 wasn't a great king. But events in his reign marked some of the biggest changes to the role of kings and queens in history.

King John

THE FEUDAL SYSTEM

After William I became king, England was governed the Norman way. That meant instead of paying rent for land, people paid with services.

At the top, barons were given land in exchange for providing knights to help the king fight his enemies. At the bottom, peasants grew crops in return for protection.

Peasant power!

THE RULES ARE CHANGED

Trouble had been brewing since the beginning of John's reign. He constantly demanded money from his barons and he misused his power as king. In 1215, the barons drew up a list of demands (called the Magna Carta) setting out what the king could and couldn't do.

Sign NOW! Or we make trouble BIG TIME

Alright! Alright! I'll sign

THE DEAL

Eventually the Magna Carta was signed at Runnymede, exactly halfway between Windsor Castle where the king was staying and where the barons were camped.

Tea breaks!

Comfy beds!

LOVE STORIES

Royal marriages were once arranged so that powerful families were brought together to rule over large territories. Love didn't get a look-in!

A STORMY MARRIAGE
Henry II married Eleanor of Aquitaine in 1152. They were both clever, hot tempered and quarrelled all the time. Eleanor encouraged their sons to rebel against their father. Henry felt so threatened by her that at the end of his life, he kept her under house arrest.

A BAD MATCH
George IV was forced to marry Caroline of Brunswick. They couldn't stand each other. When George was crowned in 1821, Caroline turned up for the Coronation. But guards stopped her entering Westminster Abbey!

OFF TO A SHAKY START
Mary II was a tall 15-year-old when she was sent to the Netherlands to marry her older, shorter cousin William in 1677. It was an unlikely match but over time they grew to love each other. William was heartbroken when Mary died of smallpox.

Is this him?

FIND OUT MORE about William and Mary on page 33

LUCKY IN LOVE

There have been many happy royal marriages. Elizabeth II's parents, King George VI and Queen Elizabeth (later The Queen Mother), were famously well matched.

Elizabeth II and Prince Philip, Duke of Edinburgh, were happily married for 73 years until Prince Philip's death in 2021.

King George VI

A DIFFICULT CHOICE

George VI never expected to become king but his brother, the future Edward VIII, wanted to marry Wallis Simpson, a divorced American woman. Parliament said he must choose between her and the throne. Edward chose Wallis.

George VI was a shy man whose stammer made him nervous about speaking in public. His wife encouraged him to try therapy to correct it – which worked. He went on to make many successful speeches.

Do you feel nervous when you speak in front of your class?

BIG, BAD AND DANGEROUS

Henry VIII was crowned king in 1509. He was tall, handsome, rich and powerful. What a catch! Or was he?

HENRY HAD SIX WIVES

WIFE no. 1

KATHERINE OF ARAGON

Henry was married to Katherine for more than 20 years. They had a daughter Mary (later Mary I). Henry wanted a son to succeed him. When Katherine became too old to have more children he divorced her.

WIFE no. 2

ANNE BOLEYN

Henry fell in love with Anne Boleyn while still married to Katherine. They had a daughter Elizabeth (later Elizabeth I). When Anne failed to give him a son, she was wrongly accused of having lovers, put on trial and beheaded.

HENRY VIII

MARY

EDWARD

FIND OUT MORE about Henry VIII on pages 26–27, 42–43

JANE SEYMOUR

Henry married Jane Seymour soon after Anne was executed Jane gave birth to a son, Edward (later Edward VI), but she died 12 days later.

CATHERINE HOWARD

Henry was old and fat when he married Catherine, a teenager. When Henry heard that she had a lover he had her beheaded for treason at the Tower of London.

ANNE OF CLEVES

When Henry saw a portrait of Anne he thought she looked gorgeous. But when she arrived from Germany, he decided she wasn't as attractive as he'd been led to believe. He divorced her super quick.

KATHERINE PARR

Henry married Katherine when he was near the end of his life. He wanted a friend for his final years. Henry died four years later, in 1547.

JANE SEYMOUR

ELIZABETH

The best of the Tudors!

When Henry had this picture painted, Jane was already dead.

Before the twentieth century, the Church was very important in many people's lives.

OUT!

I WANT A DIVORCE NOW!

When Henry VIII was king, most people in England were Catholics. The head of the Catholic Church is the Pope who lives in Rome, Italy. In 1527 Henry wanted a divorce from Katherine of Aragon. But he had to ask the Pope's permission.

The Pope refused so Henry broke with the Catholic Church and made himself the head of the new Church of England. That way he got the divorce he wanted.

THE DISSOLUTION OF THE MONASTERIES

Leaving the Catholic Church sparked off HUGE changes. Henry closed all the monasteries and turned out all the monks and nuns living in them. He had those who disagreed with him imprisoned or killed.

FIND OUT MORE about Henry VIII on pages 24–25

STOLEN TREASURE

Henry took away things of value in the monasteries such as lead from the roofs.

Ha! This will make the king very wealthy

I'm homeless now

I'm going back to Mum

Next in line

Henry VIII's son, Edward VI, died aged 15.

BLOODY MARY

Next in line was Henry's Catholic daughter, Mary I. She wanted to bring back the Catholic faith and punished all the people who tried to stop her. The most important people who disagreed with her were burnt at the stake. This is how she earned her nickname Bloody Mary.

Bloody Mary

FIND OUT MORE about Mary I on pages 11, 24

THE FIRST ELIZABETH

When Mary I died in 1558, her half-sister Elizabeth became queen. Under her rule, England overcame powerful enemies and saw some of the greatest events in its history.

Elizabeth I as a young queen

Elizabeth invited the best musicians, poets and playwrights (including William Shakespeare) to perform for her.

Lizzie loves a bit of bling

FAME AND FORTUNE

Francis Drake, a daring sea captain, undertook great sea voyages around the world. He had his eyes on the Spanish galleons loaded with gold shipped back to Spain from South America.

Elizabeth rewarded Sir Francis Drake with a knighthood.

FIND OUT MORE about Elizabeth I on pages 15, 24

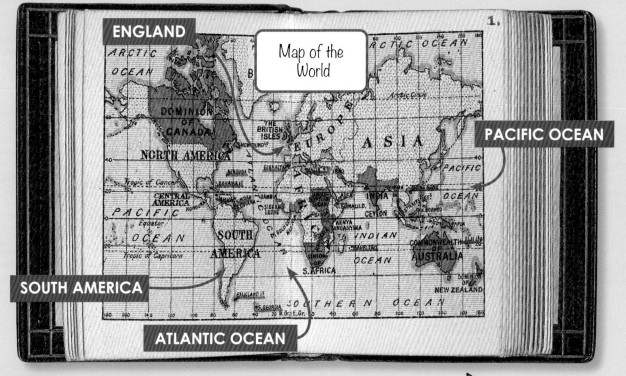

ENGLAND

Map of the World

PACIFIC OCEAN

SOUTH AMERICA

ATLANTIC OCEAN

A GREAT SEAMAN

In 1577 Drake set sail. He crossed the Atlantic, then sailed up the west coast of South America to plunder Spanish ports and ships. He sailed back to England across the Pacific Ocean. It meant that Drake was the first English person to sail around the world.

Mary, Queen of Scots

A RIVAL QUEEN

Mary, Queen of Scots fled to England when Scottish nobles forced her to give up the Scottish throne. Elizabeth was worried. Mary was her cousin and next in line to the English throne. Would she try to overthrow her?

Ordering the death of another queen was a very serious matter. Elizabeth struggled with what to do for a long time. Finally, she reluctantly signed Mary's death warrant.

TROUBLE AHEAD

Elizabeth I never married and had no children to succeed her. When she died in 1603, James, the son of Mary, Queen of Scots, became James VI of Scotland and James I of England.

Charles I

WHAT I SAY GOES!

James became the first person to rule England and Scotland together. He was succeeded by his son, Charles I, in 1625. James and Charles both believed that nobody had the right to question what they did or why they did it because God had chosen them to rule.

I'll show them how to do it

CIVIL WAR

Charles's idea of how the country should be ruled was very different from many people in Parliament. The quarrel between king and Parliament slowly got worse until finally in 1642, it exploded into a civil war (a war between people of the same country).

Oliver Cromwell

ROUNDHEADS VS CAVALIERS

Oliver Cromwell, an English general, was in charge of those on the side of Parliament (Roundheads). They eventually won against the Royalists (Cavaliers).

FIND OUT MORE about the Civil War on page 38

ENGLAND WITHOUT A KING

Oliver Cromwell governed the country as Lord Protector for five years. He wanted to destroy anything to do with kingship – including the king himself.

SENTENCED TO DEATH!

Charles was put on trial and sentenced to death. This picture shows Charles's execution in front of the Banqueting House in London.

Charles was buried at Windsor Castle where his head was reattached to his body.

I'll have him put back together in no time!

CAN YOU SPOT?

◆ A man who has turned away in tears
◆ Someone holding Charles's severed head
◆ Two people standing on boxes for a better view

BANCKET HAVS.

GOD SAVE THE KING

After Cromwell died, Parliament eventually decided to bring back Charles I's eldest son, also called Charles, from France where he had been banished. He was crowned Charles II in 1661 but kings and queens were never as powerful again.

I'm gonna have some fun

Charles II was a very popular king. He loved sport and took a great interest in science, art and architecture. He was nicknamed the Merry Monarch.

Awesome!

NO MORE CATHOLIC RULERS

Charles I's second son, James, was a Catholic. He inherited the throne as James II of England and James VII of Scotland in 1685. But no one wanted a Catholic king.

WHAT TO DO?

In 1688, important people decided to invite William of Orange (a Protestant prince from the Netherlands) to rule rather than a Catholic king.

NO FIGHTING!

William landed in Devon with 250 ships and marched to London. Meanwhile James fled to France. Parliament agreed that William and Mary, the daughter of James II, should rule together. Parliament also agreed that no Catholic prince or princess could become king or queen again.

This gold medal celebrated the Coronation of William III and Mary II.

CAN YOU SPOT?

◆ In the top half, ships setting sail from Holland
◆ In the bottom half, ships arriving at Brixham in Devon

TEARS AND FEARS

Being king or queen doesn't mean your life is problem-free. Throughout history some rulers have found it hard to fit in with friends or family. Others have suffered sickness, personal tragedy or loneliness.

I wish I was as popular as Sarah …

BESTIE OR BULLY?

Queen Anne came to the throne in 1702. Anne's best friend was Sarah Churchill, the Duchess of Marlborough. Sarah was glamorous and popular – Anne adored her. Sadly, Sarah probably took advantage of this and used her power to control Anne.

Anne was poorly educated, shy and short-sighted.

GREAT BRITAIN

Even so, Anne was popular and her reign was a success. Scotland voted to join England and Wales in 1707 so she was the first monarch to rule the newly created British nation.

'SPRECHEN SIE DEUTSCH?'

Anne had 17 children but they all died young so the throne passed to her German cousin, George I, at her death.

George I didn't speak English and very few of his ministers spoke German. So the business of running the country was left to Parliament. George's chief minister, Sir Robert Walpole, became the first prime minister and went to live at 10 Downing Street. Prime ministers still live there today.

George I

I just shout

What's he saying?

No idea

George II was crowned in 1727. He was ruler of Hanover, part of Germany, but he never visited the country!

Do you, your friends or neighbours speak English as your first language?

HAPPY FAMILIES

King George III and Queen Charlotte married in 1761 and were devoted to each other. They loved to escape stuffy London court life and go to Kew Palace with their children at weekends. There, the family led a simple life, taking lots of exercise and eating plenty of vegetables.

This ring with a portrait of George III belonged to Queen Charlotte.

You've got the puppy

I wanted to hold the parrot

George and Charlotte with their six eldest children

A VERY LARGE FAMILY

George and Charlotte had 15 children – larger than any other British royal family. All of them except Octavius and Alfred grew to be adults.

Can you number the royal children's silver spoons in the order that they were born?

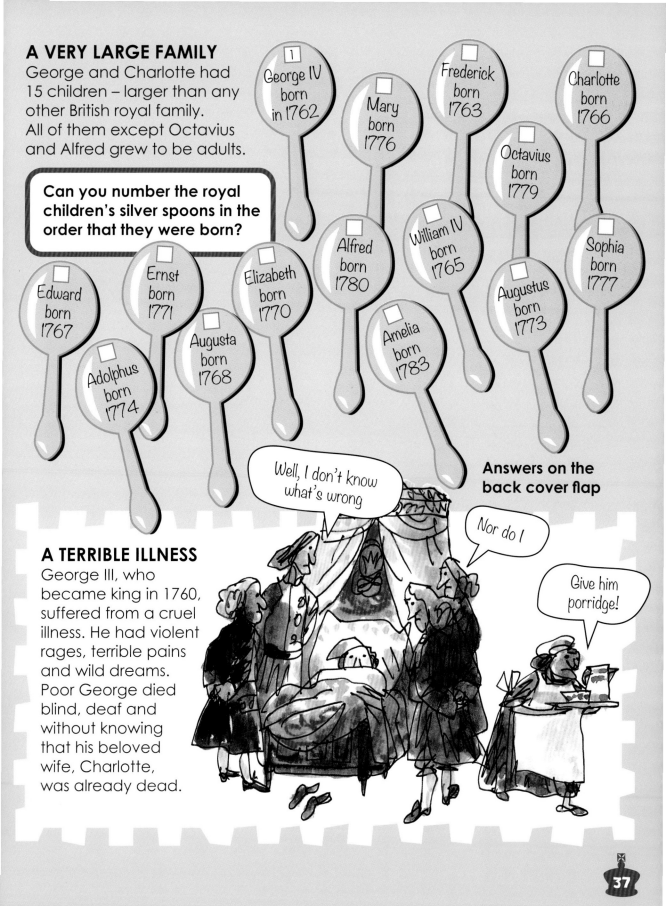

Answers on the back cover flap

A TERRIBLE ILLNESS

George III, who became king in 1760, suffered from a cruel illness. He had violent rages, terrible pains and wild dreams. Poor George died blind, deaf and without knowing that his beloved wife, Charlotte, was already dead.

MY PETS ARE MY BESTIES

'BOY' THE WONDER DOG

Boy was a hunting poodle given to Prince Rupert (nephew of Charles I) for company when he was imprisoned fighting in Europe. Once back in England, Boy followed Prince Rupert into battle during the English Civil War.

One of the first pets kept at Windsor Castle was a parrot belonging to Richard II's young queen, Isabella.

Prince Rupert was a Cavalier.

Boy was killed after he escaped his leash and chased after his master into the Battle of Marston Moor in 1644.

My master is the best

Do you have a pet? If not, what would you choose?

It was said that Boy could find hidden treasure. WHAT A DOG!

TREASURE

FIND OUT MORE about the Civil War on page 30

DOGS AND PONIES

Princess Victoria (later Queen Victoria) had few friends so she was especially fond of animals. She had a dog called Dash and a pony called Rosy.

Not again!

Victoria liked to dress Dash in a red jacket and blue trousers.

Dash, a Cavalier King Charles spaniel

FIND OUT MORE about Princess Victoria on page 40

Princess Elizabeth (later Elizabeth II)

Princess Margaret

FAVOURITE DOGS

Elizabeth II loved corgis! She got her first corgi, Dookie, when she was seven and she had more than 30 during her lifetime. She loved horses too and aged four learnt to ride her Shetland pony called Peggy.

FIND OUT MORE about Elizabeth II on pages 4–6, 23

LONELY VICKY

A DREARY CHILDHOOD
Victoria's childhood was a strict round of lessons and exercise organised by her mother and her mother's adviser – whom she hated. When Victoria became queen in 1837, aged 18, she was determined to escape both of them.

STRICT RULES
Victoria was rarely allowed to be alone as a child. She slept in the same room as her mother and never came downstairs without holding someone's hand.

IMAGINARY FRIENDS
Victoria invented a make-believe world around her collection of 132 wooden dolls.

Hold tight!

I wanna do this myself!

Do you have a secret world? Or an imaginary friend?

HAPPY TO HELP

When Victoria became queen aged 18 she knew nothing about ruling the country. She turned to her prime minister, Lord Melbourne, for help. He acted like a father and advised her on her duties as a queen.

Lord Melbourne

Victoria held her first meeting with senior advisers and ministers just five hours after becoming queen.

PRINCE ALBERT

When Victoria was 17 she fell in love with her German cousin, Prince Albert of Saxe-Coburg and Gotha. She married him three years after becoming queen and they had nine children. Albert died unexpectedly in 1861. Victoria was heartbroken and was in mourning for 40 years until she died in 1901, at the age of 81.

MOHAMMED ABDUL KARIM

In the last years of her life Victoria became very fond of Mohammed Abdul Karim, an Indian attendant. Victoria made him her trusted adviser, which annoyed the people of her court. After her death he was sent back to India and all his books and possessions were destroyed.

Mohammed Abdul Karim

FIND OUT MORE about Queen Victoria on page 39

IN IT TO WIN IT

Most of us like to be seen as clever, or very good at art, music or sport. Kings and queens are no different.

Henry VIII's tilting armour

I'M THE WINNER!

Henry VIII was a great sportsman when he was young. He loved to outdo everyone when hunting, wrestling, playing tennis, taking part in mock battles called tilts – and even dancing.

THE FIELD OF CLOTH OF GOLD

Henry's great rival was the French king, Francis I. In 1520, an important meeting to agree peace between France and England took place in France. No money was spared as the two kings tried to outdo each other!

The meeting became known as **THE FIELD OF CLOTH OF GOLD**.

CAN YOU SPOT?

◆ Henry on horseback painted a bit bigger than anyone else
◆ A fountain flowing with wine
◆ Tents made of gold cloth

Windsor Castle was built close to a forest where only kings, queens and invited nobles could hunt.

THE HUNT
In the past, hunting was the top sport for kings and queens. Henry VIII hunted every day except on holy days. His first two wives, Katherine of Aragon and Anne Boleyn, often went with him. His daughter, Princess Elizabeth (later Elizabeth I), loved to hunt too.

*No puddings, presents or holly
No Christmas, merry or jolly*

When Oliver Cromwell became Lord Protector he banned all sport, entertainment and even Christmas. SPOIL SPORT!

GOLDEN PALACES

When George IV came to the throne in 1820, Britain was becoming more and more powerful and wealthy by ruling other countries and through developments in industry and technology.

CANDLESTICKS
This candlestick holder is part of an enormous golden dinner service which George IV covered with even more gold.

EASTER EGG
George V bought this Easter egg decorated with patterns made in gold, platinum and set with precious and semi-precious jewels and pearls.

GOLD, GOLD AND MORE GOLD
George IV wanted his palaces to impress other rulers and important people. He enlarged Buckingham Palace and had as many rooms as possible decorated with loads of gold. Then he filled it with his huge collection of priceless paintings and expensive furniture and ornaments.

Many other members of the royal family loved to collect precious objects too.

BOAT-SHAPED POT

George IV bought this precious container to hold sweet-smelling dried flowers. It was made over 250 years ago and cost as much then as an expensive car today.

PIANO

Queen Victoria and Prince Albert enjoyed playing the piano and singing. They had this grand piano made for Buckingham Palace.

CHINESE VASE

George IV displayed this rare Chinese vase with a gold-covered handle and legs at Windsor Castle.

Just a little more gold I think

People joked that if someone stood still for long enough George IV would have them covered in gold!

WINDSOR CASTLE

George IV didn't stop there. He had Windsor Castle made to look grander by raising the height of the Round Tower and the surrounding castle walls. Inside, he covered as much as possible with real gold.

THE FUTURE IS HERE

When King Charles III came to the throne, his eldest son Prince William became Prince of Wales. He will become the next king.

The Prince and Princess of Wales joining in on a training day for runners taking part in the 2017 London Marathon.

Join us to save the world!

HELPING OTHERS
The Prince of Wales is married to Catherine, The Princess of Wales. Together they help to make people aware of the big problems that affect us all such as environmental change, mental health, poverty and racism.

Do you support a special cause or charity?

The sea was so murky it was like swimming in lentil soup!

SPORTY SORTS

Many of our recent kings and queens have been good at sports. George V loved sailing, Edward VIII liked golf and George VI learnt to fly. King Charles III learnt to scuba dive when he was a cadet in the Royal Navy. In 1974, he dived down to the *Mary Rose*, Henry VIII's warship, which sank in 1545.

Save our environment!

lant for e Planet

Plant more trees!

Only one Earth

Recycle

DYNASTY

NORMANS

KING OR QUEEN	IMPORTANT EVENTS
William I (the 'Conqueror')	(1066) Battle of Hastings
	(1070s–1080s) Windsor Castle built
William II ('William Rufus')	
Henry I	
Stephen and Matilda	Civil war in England

PLANTAGENETS

KING OR QUEEN	IMPORTANT EVENTS
Henry II	
Richard I ('Lionheart')	(1095–1292) The Crusades
John ('Lackland')	(1215) The Magna Carta
Henry III	(1265) First English Parliament
Edward I ('Longshanks')	(1256–1314) English campaigns to conquer Wales and Scotland
Edward II	
Edward III	(1348) The Black Death kills one-third of the population in Europe
Richard II	(1381) The Peasants' Revolt
Henry IV	
Henry V	(1415) The Battle of Agincourt
Henry VI	
Edward IV	(1455–1485) Wars of the Roses